Loaf tin

Sandwich tin

Flan tin

Rules for success!

Measure your ingredients accurately;
use the correct size of cake tin;
use the recommended oven temperature;
use the recommended oven shelf;
AND watch your timing.

NOTE: For the purposes of this book, 1 pint is approximately 500 millilitres (*ml*), 2 pints one litre, and 1 ounce (*oz*) 25 grams (*g*). 1 inch is 2.5 centimetres (*cm*).

Contents

Acknowledgments

The author and publishers wish to acknowledge the help of EMGAS, Leicester (gas cooker); Spectrum Fabrics, Loughborough and Ashby de la Zouch (background materials); and Wrighton International Furniture, London (kitchen units) in the production of photographs for this book. Easter eggs by courtesy of Cadbury's.

Making and Decorating Cakes

by LYNNE PEEBLES

photographs by TIM CLARK

Ladybird Books Loughborough

ALL·IN·ONE METHOD

INGREDIENTS

100g (4 oz) caster sugar
100g (4 oz) soft margarine
100g (4 oz) self-raising flour
2 level teaspoonfuls baking powder
2 eggs (size 3 - 4)

EQUIPMENT

Mixing bowl
Sieve
Wooden spoon
Teaspoon
Pastry knife

1 Prepare tins if necessary. (See front of book.)

2 Put sugar, margarine and eggs in mixing bowl.

3 Sift flour with baking powder into other ingredients.

4 Beat well together for 2 – 3 minutes with a wooden spoon.

This mixture will make 2 × 18 cm (7 in) cakes or 20 small cakes in paper cake cases, or it can be cooked in a 400g (1 lb) loaf tin. With the exception of small cakes, all tins should be greased and lined as shown at front of book.

Baking times (all on middle shelf)

18 cm (7 in) cakes: 20 minutes in moderate oven – Gas Mark 4 (electricity 350°F/180°C).

Small cakes: 15 minutes at Gas Mark 5 (electricity 375°F/190°C).

Loaf tin: 50–60 minutes at Gas Mark 3 (electricity 325°F/160°C).

Loosen cakes from tins by running a knife around the edge. Turn out onto cooling rack, and cover with clean damp teatowel until cold. (This ensures cakes remain moist.)

Variations

To basic cake mixture, one of the following may be added:

Orange cake: grated rind of 1 orange.

Chocolate: 1 dessertspoonful cocoa (dissolve in 1 tablespoonful warm water).

Coffee: 1 dessertspoonful coffee powder (dissolve in 1 tablespoonful water).

Coffee and walnut: 1 dessertspoonful coffee powder (dissolve in 1 tablespoonful water), plus 50g (2 oz) chopped walnuts.

HOW TO DECORATE SIMPLY

Butter Icing

INGREDIENTS
250g (10 oz) sieved icing sugar
125g (5 oz) butter

EQUIPMENT
Small basin
Wooden spoon

1 Cream butter and sugar together until well blended (soft and creamy).
2 Cover bowl with a damp cloth until ready to use.

18 cm (7 in) cakes
Butter icing
2 cakes
2 tablespoonfuls jam or lemon curd

Loaf tin
Butter icing
Cake sliced into 3 layers
2 tablespoonfuls lemon curd or jam for centre
Glacé cherries and angelica

Use fork to decorate top

Use a fork to decorate sides and top

Butterfly Cakes

1 Bake 20 small cakes as shown on page 4, and prepare butter icing.

2 Cut a circle from the top of each cake, then cut circle in half for two 'wings'.

3 Spoon some butter icing on top of each cake, and place wings on top of icing. Decorate with half a walnut.

To flavour icing

Orange: add 3 teaspoonfuls of fresh orange juice.

Chocolate: add 1 dessertspoonful cocoa powder (dissolve in 1 tablespoonful of warm water) or 50g (2 oz) melted chocolate. Decorate with grated chocolate.

Coffee: add 1 dessertspoonful coffee powder (dissolved in 1 tablespoonful of water). Decorate with chocolate buttons.

Coffee and walnut: add 1 dessertspoonful of coffee powder (dissolved in 1 tablespoonful of water). Decorate with chopped or halved walnuts.

7

CREAMING METHOD

This is the traditional method for making a light, rich
cake and there are many ways of using the basic
mixture.

INGREDIENTS
100g (4 oz) caster sugar
100g (4 oz) margarine
100g (4 oz) self-raising flour
2 eggs (size 3–4)

EQUIPMENT
Mixing bowl
Wooden spoon
Small basin
Fork
Sieve
Tablespoon

1 Prepare tins as for all-in-one method. Put oven on.

2 Place margarine in bowl, and soften with wooden spoon.

3 Add sugar, and beat well together with wooden spoon until pale and creamy.

4 Break eggs into small basin, beat with fork.

5 Gradually add beaten egg to creamed mixture, a tablespoonful at a time, beating well with wooden spoon before each addition.

(NOTE: If egg is added too quickly, the mixture may begin to curdle. If this happens, stand bowl in hot water and beat mixture well, or add 1 tablespoonful sieved flour.)

6 When all egg has been added, gently fold in sifted flour with *metal* spoon.

7 Bake as for all-in-one method.

Traditional Victoria Sandwich

1 Divide basic creamed mixture between 2 greased and
  lined 18 cm (7 in) tins, and bake.

2 Sandwich cakes together with 2 tablespoonfuls
  plum jam.

3 Sprinkle top with caster sugar.

Variations

To basic creamed mixture, you can add any one of the following, or any of the flavourings suggested for the all-in-one method cakes.

Lemon cake: grated rind of 1 lemon.

Almond cake: 50g (2 oz) ground almonds and a few drops almond essence.

Light Fruit Cake

Bake in a deep 18 cm (7 in) cake tin, or 400g (1 lb) loaf tin. Add 25g (1 oz) chopped glacé cherries, 25g (1 oz) sultanas, 25g (1 oz) raisins and 25g (1 oz) currants (or 100g (4 oz) mixed dried fruit).

To decorate light fruit cake you can sprinkle the top of the mixture with sugar before baking, or you can use glacé icing, as described on the next page.

GLACE ICING

This is a water icing, and exact measurement of water and icing sugar is essential. This icing is not used for the centre of cake but for top, or top and sides.

INGREDIENTS
150g (6 oz) icing sugar
6 teaspoonfuls cold water

EQUIPMENT
Basin
Wooden spoon
Teaspoon
Sieve

Sieve icing sugar, add water, and mix well with wooden spoon until mixture will fall off spoon and find its own level in bowl. If more water is needed, add drop by drop.

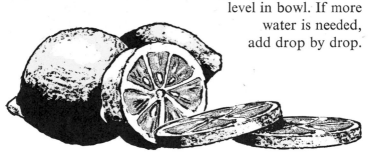

Lemon Icing

Mix icing sugar with lemon juice in place of water, and add a few drops of yellow food colouring.
Sandwich cakes together (or split into layers) and fill with lemon curd.
Place on cooling rack and pour glacé icing on top.
Allow to run down sides. Leave 2–3 minutes, then move onto serving plate before icing sets.

Almond Icing

Sandwich cakes together (or split into layers), and fill with apricot jam.

Make up glacé icing, adding a few drops of almond essence. Place cake on cooling rack and pour icing over it. Leave 2–3 minutes, then move onto serving plate and decorate top with blanched, flaked, chopped or toasted almonds. (To blanch almonds, put into boiling water for a minute, transfer to cold water, then rub off skins with your fingers.)

FEATHER ICING

This is a technique of applying glacé icing which requires a steady hand and a flat surface to work on. It can be used on any 18 cm (7 in) layered or sandwich cake after filling. The base of the cake is often used as the flat top surface. Choose any of the recipes given for the all-in-one method or creamed mixtures (with the exception of the light fruit cake).

INGREDIENTS
100g (4 oz) icing sugar
3 – 4 teaspoonfuls water
Few drops food colouring

EQUIPMENT
Greaseproof paper
Pointed knife
Scissors

To make an icing bag, cut a 25 cm (10 in) square of greaseproof paper, fold it in half diagonally and cut across fold. Using one half, fold as shown, and open into cone. Snip 1–2 millimetres off end.

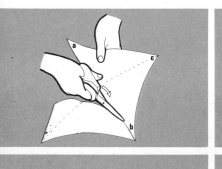

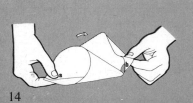

Mix sieved icing sugar and water, and beat well together. Remove 1 tablespoonful and to it add a few drops of food colouring (this is for the piped icing). The consistency of the icing should be such that it just finds its own level, *slightly* stiffer than for ordinary glacé icing. Place filled cake on serving plate.

Working quickly, spread white icing on cake top, taking it just to the edge (any drips can be removed when icing has set). Snip off base of icing bag and pipe lines of coloured icing across cake. Score across lines with sharp knife, turn cake and score the opposite way. Leave to set.

Jewel Cakes

INGREDIENTS

50 g (2 oz) caster sugar
50 g (2 oz) margarine or butter
50 g (2 oz) self-raising flour
1 egg

Glacé icing

100 g (4 oz) icing sugar
4 teaspoonfuls cold water

Decoration

Glacé cherries
Angelica
Chocolate buttons
Walnut halves
Sugar strands
12 cake cases

1 Make up the cake mixture using the creaming method. (*See* page 8.)

2 Bake in an 18 cm (7 in) square cake tin for 20–25 minutes.

3 Remove from the tin, cover in a clean damp teatowel, and cool.

4 Make up the glacé icing. (*See* page 12.)

5 Pour the icing mixture on the top of the cake and spread it to the edges with a palette knife.

6 Before the icing is set, cut the cake into twelve pieces and decorate each one.

7 Place each in a cake case and serve.

WHISKED CAKES

These cakes contain no fat and do not generally store or keep very well.

(true sponge cakes)

EQUIPMENT
Mixing bowl
Rotary whisk
Tablespoon
Sieve
Baking tin (flan, Swiss roll or 18 cm (7 in) round tin)

INGREDIENTS
(for small Swiss roll or sponge flan)
2 eggs *(size 2–3)*
62½g *(2½ oz) caster sugar*
50g *(2 oz) plain flour*

INGREDIENTS
(for large Swiss roll or 2-layer sponge cake)
3 eggs *(size 2–3)*
87½g *(3½ oz) caster sugar*
75g *(3 oz) plain flour*

Baking times:
small Swiss roll
        8 – 10 minutes
sponge flan
        – 12 minutes
sponge cakes
        10 – 15 minutes
large Swiss roll
        – 12 minutes

1 Grease and line tins – this mixture will not wait.

2 Put oven on at Gas Mark 6 (electricity 400°F/200°C).

3 Put eggs and sugar in a mixing bowl. Whisk steadily for 8 – 10 minutes. The mixture will lighten in colour and should hold a trail for 10 seconds.
   (See photograph bottom left.)

(NOTE: On a cold day the sugar can be warmed to speed up mixing.)

4 Sift in flour gently but quickly, then, using a figure of eight movement, fold in flour with *metal* spoon. This stage should take about 30 seconds.
   Pour immediately into prepared baking tin in oven.

Swiss Roll

INGREDIENTS
(in addition to basic mixture for either small or large Swiss roll)
$12\frac{1}{2}g$ ($\frac{1}{2}$ oz) sugar
2–3 tablespoonfuls jam

EQUIPMENT
1 sheet greaseproof paper
Sharp knife
Palette or pastry knife
Swiss roll tin

1 While Swiss roll is baking, place clean damp teatowel on work surface. On top of this place the greaseproof paper, and sprinkle with sugar.

2 Soften jam in a small basin with a knife.

3 When Swiss roll is cooked, turn immediately upside down onto paper. Remove tin and paper – tearing from centre to sides.

4 Trim off all edges with a sharp knife, cutting straight down *not* sawing.

5 Spread jam over surface to within 1 cm ($\frac{1}{2}$ in) of each edge. Make cut almost through 1 cm ($\frac{1}{2}$ in) away from one short edge. Fold over along this line, lifting cake with greaseproof paper. Roll up to end and hold in place for 1 minute with edge at base.

Sponge Flan

Bake sponge flan as on page 18. When cooked, free edges using a straight knife and knocking the flan gently from side to side in the tin. Turn onto a cooling rack. Cool. Place on serving plate, and fill with fruit. Glaze and decorate.

Filling and Glazing

INGREDIENTS
(in addition to
basic mixture)
*3 level teaspoonfuls
arrowroot*
Large tin peaches
*125 ml ($\frac{1}{4}$ pint) water
or juice from fruit*
*25 g (1 oz) sugar
if using water only*
Few drops of food colouring

1 Put arrowroot in a small pan and gradually blend in water and sugar, or fruit juice.

2 Heat to boiling point, stirring all the time with a *wooden* spoon.

3 Boil for one minute until clear and thickened, then remove from heat and add food colouring. Cool slightly and use back of wooden spoon to trail glaze over fruit to be covered.

Sponge Cakes

Fill and decorate using any of the ideas given for all-in-one or creamed cakes. Sponge cakes *can* be flavoured but only within certain limits. For example, for a chocolate sponge, replace 12½ g (½ oz) flour with 12½ g (½ oz) cocoa, sifting it with the flour before adding, and for a coffee sponge, replace 12½ g (½ oz) flour with 12½ g (½ oz) coffee powder, again sifting it with the flour before adding.

Orange Sunshine Cake

Basic recipe for whisked sponge (using 3 eggs), adding the finely-grated rind of an orange.

Glacé icing

125 g (5 oz) icing sugar
5 teaspoonfuls
orange juice
A few drops of orange
food colouring

Filling

125 g (5 oz) lemon curd
or apricot jam

1 Make sponge cake using whisking method (*see* page 18), but add grated rind before the flour.
2 Pour into 2 prepared 18 cm (7 in) cake tins.

3 Bake at Gas Mark 6 (electricity 400°F/200°C) for 15 minutes.

4 Cool slightly and remove from the tins, cover with a clean damp teatowel and leave until cool.

5 Sandwich cake together with filling. Put on a plate.

6 Make up the glacé icing (*see* page 12), adding the orange juice. Remove 1 tablespoonful of icing and colour with the orange food colouring. Pour the uncoloured icing onto the centre of the cake. Allow to spread but not to set. Pour the coloured icing on the top of the cake in the centre and draw out the rays of the sun with a sharp knife. Leave to set.

MELTED CAKES

Gingerbread

INGREDIENTS
250 g (10 oz) plain flour
1 rounded teaspoonful ground ginger
1 rounded teaspoonful bicarbonate of soda
Good pinch of salt
100 g (4 oz) sugar
75 g (3 oz) margarine
75 g (3 oz) black treacle
75 g (3 oz) golden syrup
125 ml ($\frac{1}{4}$ pint) milk
1 small egg

1 Prepare an 18–20 cm (7–8 in) deep tin, grease and line.

2 Sift dry ingredients, except sugar, into mixing bowl.

3 Place golden syrup, black treacle, margarine and sugar in pan and heat gently until all are melted together. Cool for five minutes.

4 Add melted ingredients to dry ingredients – rinse pan out with milk – add milk and egg to bowl.

5 Beat well with wooden spoon. Pour into prepared tin. Bake at Gas Mark 3 (electricity 325°F/160°C) for 1 hour or until firm.

Gingerbread can be decorated with glacé icing (100 g (4 oz) icing).

Oat Gingerbread

Replace 50 g (2 oz) flour with 50 g (2 oz) rolled oats for a coarser textured result.

Fruit Gingerbread

To basic recipe, add 50–75 g (2–3 oz) raisins or sultanas.

RUBBED-IN CAKES

These are less rich cakes that tend not to keep very well. They are, however, very quick to prepare and easy to make.

Plain Cake

INGREDIENTS
200 g (8 oz) self-raising flour
Pinch of salt
100 g (4 oz) sugar
100 g (4 oz) margarine
1 egg (size 2–3)
Milk to mix
Few drops vanilla essence

EQUIPMENT
Sieve
Mixing bowl
Pastry knife
18 cm (7 in) cake tin
or 400 g (1 lb) loaf tin,
greased and lined
Fork
Small basin

1 Sift flour and salt into bowl, add sugar. Coat margarine in flour, cut up into small pieces, and rub in. If baking a variation, add any additional ingredients at this stage.

2 Beat egg in small basin, add vanilla essence. Add to rubbed-in mixture with enough milk to make a mixture which falls from spoon in lumps.

3 Place in cake tin.

4 Bake at Gas Mark 3 (electricity 325°F/160°C) for approximately one hour.

Everyday Fruit Cake

To basic recipe, add 100 g (4 oz) mixed dried fruit, 25 g (1 oz) glacé cherries and 1 level teaspoonful mixed spice. Bake as before.

Cherry and Coconut Cake

To basic recipe, add 100 g (4 oz) glacé cherries, washed and quartered and coated in 50 g (2 oz) desiccated coconut (additional milk may be needed).

Banana and Apple Cake

To basic recipe, add 1 sliced banana, 1 chopped apple, 25 g (1 oz) raisins and 25 g (1 oz) chopped cherries. Bake as before.

SPECIAL SMALL CAKES

Apricot Baskets

EQUIPMENT
10–12 cake cases
Greaseproof paper
Scissors
No. 8 or no. 14 icing nozzle

INGREDIENTS
(to make 10–12 cakes)
Half basic recipe for all-in-one or creamed mixture
1 large tin apricot halves
3 level teaspoonfuls arrowroot + few drops food colouring or packet orange Quick-Jel
Angelica strips
Butter icing or fresh cream

1 Follow method for basic mixture, divide between 10–12 cake cases, and bake for 15 minutes.

2 Cool. Level off tops if necessary.

3 Make up glaze. Place arrowroot in small pan, gradually add 125 ml ($\frac{1}{4}$ pint) fruit juice, and bring to boil, stirring all the time until thickened and clear. Remove from heat, and add food colouring (or follow packet instructions for Quick-Jel).

4 Dip each apricot in the glaze, and place one on top of each cake. Pipe cream round edge of each cake. (*See* pages 32 & 33.)

5 Cut thin strips of angelica to form handles, and serve.

Jam Cakes

INGREDIENTS

(for 10–12) *Half basic
recipe for all-in-one
or creamed mixture*

*10–12 teaspoonfuls jam
(assorted flavours if wished)*

*Butter icing made from
100 g (4 oz) icing sugar
and 50 g (2 oz) butter*

EQUIPMENT

10–12 cake cases
Greaseproof paper
Scissors
No. 8 or no. 14 icing nozzle

1 Follow method for basic
mixture. Divide between
10–12 cake cases and bake
for 15 minutes.

2 Cool. Level off tops if
necessary.

3 Make butter icing.

4 Make piping bag using
25 cm (10 in) square of
greaseproof paper,
following instructions on
page 14.

5 Snip off 1 cm ($\frac{1}{2}$ in) from
end of bag. Put in nozzle,

then place butter icing in the bag. Fold over end.

6 Pipe a border around each cake and place a teaspoonful of jam in the centre of each.

How to pipe

Hold the top of the bag firmly with your right hand and the centre with your left, keeping the bag upright. The action is to squeeze (with the whole of your left hand), then stop, then lift. If you think, 'Squeeze, stop, lift,' each time, then you will find improvement comes with practice.

NOTE:

If it is your first attempt at piping, make up two bags from the square of greaseproof and use the first one to practise piping the butter icing onto a clean plate. You can then put it into the second bag and use it on the cakes. It may take a few minutes longer, but the effort is worth the better results. Simple piping around the edge makes a world of difference to these cakes.

CHEESE CAKE

Although not a cake in the true sense, a cheesecake makes a delicious dessert or tea-time treat.

INGREDIENTS
100 g (4 oz) crushed digestive biscuits
50 g (2 oz) butter
350 g (14 oz) cottage cheese
3 eggs
100 g (4 oz) caster sugar
1 rounded tablespoonful cornflour
Finely-grated rind of 1 lemon
4 tablespoonfuls top of the milk
125 ml (¼ pint) double or whipping cream

1 Melt the butter over a low heat.

2 Remove from the heat and mix in the crushed biscuits. Press into the base of the tin.

3 Rub the cottage cheese through a sieve, using a tablespoon.

4 Add the egg yolks, cornflour, 75 g (3 oz) of the sugar, lemon rind and the top of the milk. Mix well together.

5 Whisk the egg whites until stiff, then whisk in the remaining 25 g (1 oz) sugar.

6 Fold into the cheese mixture, using a tablespoon.

7 Pour onto the biscuit base in the tin. Bake at Gas Mark 2 (electricity 300°F/150°C) for 1 hour 15 minutes.

8 Leave in the oven to cool.

9 Remove from the tin when cold. Decorate with whipped cream and lemon butterflies.

SPECIAL LARGE CAKES

Chocolate Gâteau

INGREDIENTS

150 g (6 oz) caster sugar
150 g (6 oz) margarine
150 g (6 oz) self-raising flour
3 eggs (size 3)
1 tablespoonful cocoa
(dissolve in 1 tablespoonful hot water)

Butter icing
300 g (12 oz) icing sugar
150 g (6 oz) butter
1 tablespoonful cocoa
(dissolve in 1 tablespoonful hot water)

Decorations

100–150 g (4–6 oz) chocolate vermicelli (sugar strands).
Chocolate buttons or chocolate flake.

Follow method for either all-in-one or creamed mixture.
Bake in two 18 or 20 cm (7 or 8 in) greased and lined
cake tins for 20 to 25 minutes at Gas Mark 4 (electricity
350°F/180°C).

1 Make butter icing.

2 Sandwich cakes together with a small amount of butter
  icing, spreading some of the icing around sides.

3 Place sugar strands on greaseproof paper. Then, using
  both hands – one on top, one on base – turn cake
  around so that sides become covered in sugar strands.

4 Put on serving plate, and sprinkle top of cake with
  icing sugar.

5 Put remaining icing in an icing bag with a no. 8 or 14
  nozzle, and pipe border. Then pipe from side to side
  across cake.

6 Finish with large swirl in centre, and decorate with
  buttons or flake.

Mandarin and Grape Gâteau

INGREDIENTS

1 basic whisked mixture using 3 eggs (size 2–3) (cook in greased and lined 800 g (2 lb) loaf tin)

2–3 tablespoonfuls apricot jam

100 g (4 oz) desiccated coconut

1 tin mandarin oranges

50 g (2 oz) black grapes

125 ml ($\frac{1}{4}$ pint) fresh double (or whipping) cream

(NOTE: Butter cream made with 125 g (5 oz) icing sugar 50 g (2 oz) butter and 1 tablespoonful fruit juice may be used instead of fresh cream.)

1 Make cake, using whisking method. Cover and allow to cool, then slice into three layers, lengthways.

2 Meanwhile drain mandarin oranges, wash grapes and cut in half, taking out pips.

3 Whip fresh cream until stiff enough to stand in soft peaks (or make up butter icing).

4 Place coconut on an ovenproof shallow dish under a hot grill, and turn frequently until evenly brown.

5 Spread a thin layer of cream and apricot jam between the cake layers and cover the sides with cream. Carefully dip the sides in the toasted coconut, then put cake on to serving plate.

6 Put cream in icing bag.

7 Arrange mandarins and grapes attractively along top of the cake.

8 Pipe a border along top edges of cake.

Fruit remaining can be arranged at the base of the cake.

Mint Chocolate
Birthday Cake

INGREDIENTS

150 g (6 oz) caster sugar
150 g (6 oz) margarine
150 g (6 oz) self-raising flour
3 eggs (size 3)
Green food colouring
Half teaspoonful peppermint essence
2 dessertspoonfuls cocoa
1 tablespoonful hot water

For icing and decoration:
350 g (14 oz) icing sugar
125 g (5 oz) butter
2 dessertspoonfuls cocoa
1 tablespoonful hot water
150 g (6 oz) chocolate sugar strands

EQUIPMENT

2 × 18 cm (7 in) tins greased and lined

1 Make cake mixture using all-in-one or creaming method. Transfer half mixture to another bowl, and add cocoa and water. Mix well.

2 To the other half of mixture add food colouring and peppermint essence.

3 Bake. Cover and cool.

4 Using 250 g (10 oz) icing sugar and butter, make up butter icing and flavour with half the cocoa. Sandwich cakes together with icing and spread remaining icing over sides taking it just over top edge. Coat sides in chocolate sugar strands and place on serving plate.

5 Make up glacé icing with remaining 100 g (4 oz) icing sugar. Remove 1 tablespoonful and colour green, then place in paper icing bag (either fit no. 2 writing nozzle or simply snip off the end of the bag). Flavour rest of glacé icing with cocoa.

6 Pour chocolate glacé icing on top of cake. When set, pipe *Happy Birthday* with green icing. Arrange candles in butter icing at edge, and serve.

Easter Cake *(Simnel cake)*

INGREDIENTS

400 g (1 lb) mixed dried fruit
200 g (8 oz) plain flour
Pinch of salt
1 level teaspoonful cinnamon
1 level teaspoonful ground nutmeg
150 g (6 oz) margarine
150 g (6 oz) brown sugar
3 eggs (size 3)
1 tablespoonful apricot jam
400 g (1 lb) marzipan
Piece of wide ribbon

1 Grease and line a deep 18 cm (7 in) cake tin.

2 Divide the marzipan into three (one piece should be slightly smaller than the others).

3 Cream margarine and sugar well together, and gradually add eggs (as for creamed mixture, page 8). Fold in the flour, sieve with spice, and finally add the dried fruit.

4 Place half the cake mixture in tin. Roll out one third of marzipan and put on top of mixture. Put remaining cake mixture on top of marzipan.

5 Bake cake at Gas Mark 3 (electricity 325°F/160°C) for 2–2½ hours until all sound of bubbling has stopped. (It is not possible to test with a skewer because of the layer of marzipan.) Leave to cool in tin.

6 Take second (larger) piece of marzipan and roll out to shape of tin. Brush cake with apricot jam, and press marzipan in place. Remove from tin.

7 Out of the last (smaller) piece of marzipan shape 11 eggs. Brush marzipan top with jam. Put eggs in place, and decorate edges. Place under grill until evenly brown.

8 Tie a ribbon round the side, and serve.

If you wish you can decorate your Easter cake with some 'nests' instead of just eggs, or these can be put into small cake cases and served on their own at tea time.
(*See* page 44.)

Easter Nests

INGREDIENTS
100–150 g (4–6 oz)
chocolate
Shredded wheat – 2 pieces
Coloured sweets
Small paper cake cases

1 Melt chocolate in small
  basin over pan of boiling
  water, break up shredded
  wheat and stir in well.

2 Place in cake cases, pressing centre down to shape
  nest.

3 Leave to set in cool place and fill with coloured sweets
  or sugar eggs, or make small eggs from marzipan.

For speckled marzipan eggs, roll one end of each egg
in a little coffee powder.

CHRISTMAS CAKE

Christmas Cake

A small cake is always easier to handle than a large one, so we give two sizes and it's up to you which one you choose.

INGREDIENTS	Small cake 20 cm (8 in) round (18 cm (7 in) square)	Larger cake 23 cm (9 in) round (20 cm (8 in) square)
Mixed dried fruit or mixed currants, raisins, sultanas	700 g (1¾ lb)	1 kilo (2½ lb)
Glacé cherries	75 g (3 oz)	100 g (4 oz)
Almonds (flaked, chopped, or ground)	50 g (2 oz)	75 g (3 oz)
Lemon rind – grated	1 teaspoonful	1 teaspoonful
Plain flour	200 g (8 oz)	300 g (12 oz)
Mixed spice	½ teaspoonful	½ teaspoonful
Cinnamon	½ teaspoonful	½ teaspoonful
Butter	150 g (6 oz)	250 g (10 oz)
Sugar (brown)	150 g (6 oz)	250 g (10 oz)
Eggs (size 2–3)	3	5
Cooking time	2½–3 hours	3½ hours
Almond paste		
Top only	300 g (¾ lb)	400 g (1 lb)
Top and sides	600–700 g (1½–1¾ lb)	700 g–1 kilo (1¾–2½ lb)

Royal icing	Small cake	Larger cake
Top only	400 g (1 lb)	500 g (1¼ lb)
Top and sides	600 g (1½ lb)	700 g (1¾ lb)
Cake board	23 cm (9 in) round	25 cm (10 in) round

Decorations

These can be bought or simply made from coloured marzipan. Ideally all the decorations on a cake should be edible, but it is really a matter of personal choice.

1 Grease and line cake tins. Oven temperatures are easily controllable these days, so there is no need to wrap brown paper around the sides of the tin.

2 Weigh out all ingredients.

3 Place butter in bowl and soften with wooden spoon; add sugar and cream well together until very soft and light. Gradually add beaten egg (if mixture begins to curdle, place bowl in hot water, or add 1 tablespoonful sieved flour and beat well in.)

4 Add the dried fruit, nuts, cherries and lemon rind and mix well in. Sift flour with spices and add to mixture. Stir well so that all ingredients are very well mixed.

If mixture is still sticking to skewer, cake is not yet cooked.

5 Place mixture in tin and slightly hollow out the centre (this ensures a flat surface after cooking).

6 Bake for required time at Gas Mark 3 (electricity 325°F/160°C) for first hour, then reduce heat to Gas Mark 2 (electricity 300°F/150°C) until cooked: use a skewer to test. Leave cake to cool in the tin.

7 Some people consider that if spirit such as brandy or sherry is added, this will improve the cake's flavour. To do this make holes with a skewer and pour spirit in. Putting it in after cooking makes sure you get flavour. If it is added during cooking, much of it evaporates and the flavour is lost.

To Decorate a Christmas Cake

The first layer is almond paste, which can either be made
to the following recipe, or bought. If buying, you will
need 300 g ($\frac{3}{4}$ lb) for the small cake, and 400 g (1 lb)
for the larger cake.

INGREDIENTS

Small cake	Larger cake
150 g (6 oz) ground almonds	*250 g (10 oz) ground almonds*
75 g (3 oz) caster sugar	*125 g (5 oz) caster sugar*
75 g (3 oz) icing sugar	*125 g (5 oz) icing sugar*
Few drops almond essence	*Few drops almond essence*
1–2 egg yolks	*2–3 egg yolks*
1 tablespoonful apricot jam	*1 tablespoonful apricot jam*

1 Mix almonds and sugar together.

2 Mix egg yolks with almond essence.

3 Mix ingredients together.
   You will find it easier to mix with your hand, which
   will soften the oils in the almonds.

4 If top of cake is uneven, trim it to sit well on the cake
   board. Either top or base of the cake can be used.

Top

5 Sprinkle work surface with sugar.
   Roll out one third of almond paste (if covering top
   and sides) to either circle or square. Brush with
   apricot jam, turn cake upside down onto almond paste,
   and press down well. Using a sharp knife, trim edges.

Sides

6 Measure round the cake with a piece of string and use this as a guide when rolling. Sprinkle work surface well with icing sugar. Keeping rest of almond paste as a long strip, roll to length of string and square off one end.

7 Brush cake sides well with apricot jam, place cake on almond paste and roll over, pressing down well. Level off other end, and press join well together until smooth. Smooth edge to top join. Place on cake board.

8 If royal icing is to be applied within 2–3 days, brush all marzipan with egg white (this stops the oils from the almonds discolouring the white icing). Alternatively, leave lightly covered for 1 week to 10 days to dry out naturally. Any pieces of marzipan left over should be stored in a polythene bag.

Royal Icing

The consistency of royal icing is very important. If it is your first attempt, a rough icing finish is easiest to achieve – but there is no reason why a little piped icing cannot be used as well for a special effect.

INGREDIENTS

Small cake
400 g (1 lb) icing sugar
2 egg whites
1 teaspoonful lemon juice
2 teaspoonfuls glycerine

Larger cake
600 g (1½ lb) icing sugar
3 egg whites
1 teaspoonful lemon juice
2 teaspoonfuls glycerine

(The glycerine will stop the icing drying out too hard.)

1 Place egg whites in mixing bowl and add lemon juice and glycerine.

2 Using a wooden spoon, gradually add the sieved icing sugar until the mixture is smooth, slightly shiny, and will stand up in soft peaks when lifted with the spoon.

3 Put icing in the centre of the top of the cake and with a pliable knife or spatula, spread the icing over the top and down the sides to the board. Using the spatula or knife, draw up the icing in soft peaks, then leave to set for 2-3 days.

4 If you are going to pipe some decorations, smooth out required area of top with a hot, dry knife.

Almond paste decorations

Using left-over almond paste, colour with green or red food colouring for holly leaves and berries, or leave uncoloured for mistletoe.
Use a tiny amount of royal icing to stick decorations in place.

FORMAL BIRTHDAY CAKE

INGREDIENTS

200 g (8 oz) caster sugar
250 g (10 oz) butter
5 eggs (size 2)
250 g (10 oz) plain flour
plus 1½ level teaspoonfuls
baking powder
50 g (2 oz) ground almonds

This uses a rich plain cake mixture which is firm enough to take marzipan and royal flat icing. It should be made 2–3 weeks before you need it.

1 Follow creaming method, sieving in flour with ground almonds.

2 Bake in a greased and lined 23 cm (9 in) deep cake tin in oven at Gas Mark 3 (electricity 325°F/160°C) for 2 hours. Cool in tin. Store for 2–3 days.

3 Cover in marzipan as for Christmas cake. Stand on cake board.

4 Make up royal icing using 600 g ($1\frac{1}{2}$ lb) icing sugar to 3 egg whites with lemon juice and glycerine. Mix until it will stand in soft peaks.

5 Spread icing round sides first of all, smoothing with straight-bladed hot knife, then leave until beginning to set.

6 Place some of remaining icing in an icing bag with a no. 2 writing nozzle and pipe a line along top outer edge.

7 To remaining icing, add more lemon until icing just finds its own level then carefully put icing on to centre of top of cake and smooth out to piped line.

8 Leave to set completely (for at least 24 hours). Any left-over icing should be stored in an airtight container.

To complete cake

Place ribbon around cake and secure with icing. Hide joining of top and sides of icing with a piped border using a no. 12 or 21 nozzle. Repeat at base of cake, joining cake to board. Add candles in holders or moulded flowers to finish.

Flowers from Icing

INGREDIENTS
100 g (4 oz) icing sugar
1 level teaspoonful powdered gelatine
1 teaspoonful water
1 heaped teaspoonful liquid glucose
Food colouring
Extra icing sugar for handling

1 Place gelatine in a mixing bowl over pan of boiling water, add the teaspoonful of water and glucose, and mix to dissolve. Remove basin from water.

2 Add food colouring and mix in icing sugar. Using your hand, gather together.

3 Shape on a sugared board, leave to dry out, and arrange on cake.

Store in an empty chocolate box or between layers of cotton wool. Shading can be achieved by painting petals with food colouring when dry.

Take four small pieces of coloured icing, shape three into flat circles and roll tiny piece to make centre.

Take four to six very small pieces of icing and flatten each one to a circle.

Put two pieces at top to form petals, and one at base.

Start with one piece and roll to a cone.

Violets

Roses

Brush with egg white and sprinkle with sugar.

Press on another piece of icing to make a second petal.

Leave to dry, then paint with food colouring.

Continue to curl pieces of icing around centre, spreading outer petals.

WHAT WENT WRONG?

What went wrong?	Why?	Next time!
Cake has a close heavy texture.	Oven temperature may have been too low or cake was cooked too near the bottom of oven.	Increase temperature and/or lift shelf.
	Insufficient cooking time.	Increase cooking time.
	The mixture was too wet.	Reduce liquid.
	Insufficient raising agent.	Check amount and increase.
Cake has a coarse open texture.	Too much raising agent.	Measure accurately and reduce.
	Uneven mixing of flour.	Mix more vigorously.
Cake sinks in middle.	Too much raising agent.	Measure accurately.
	Too much sugar.	Measure accurately.
	Overcreaming of fat and sugar.	Cream less vigorously.
	Oven temperature too low.	Increase oven temperature.
Poor shape.	Bad lining of tins, or careless filling.	Take more care.
	Wrong consistency.	Add more or less liquid as necessary.
Cracked or peaked top.	Tin too small.	Check tin size.
	Oven too hot.	Reduce oven temperature.
	Shelf too high.	Lower shelf.
Dry texture.	Insufficient liquid.	Increase liquid.
	Too much raising agent.	Measure accurately.
Hard sugary top.	Too much sugar used.	Check amount.
	Oven too slow.	Increase temperature.
	Too coarse sugar used.	Use caster sugar.
Uneven rising.	Tilted in oven.	Check oven shelves.
	Tin unevenly near source of heat.	Place centrally on oven shelves.

Faults with particular cakes

What went wrong ?	Why ?	Next time !
Rubbed-in mixtures		
Uneven texture.	Poor rubbing-in.	Rub-in more vigorously.
	Too much baking powder.	Measure accurately.
Close heavy texture.	Over rubbing-in of fat.	Rub-in less vigorously.
Dry texture.	Over cooking.	Reduce cooking time.
	Too little liquid.	Add more liquid.
Melted mixtures		
Close heavy texture.	Too much syrup or treacle.	Weigh very carefully.
	Over-beating after adding liquid (will also give shiny top).	Don't beat so much.
Creamed mixtures		
Close heavy texture.	Insufficient creaming of fat and sugar.	Cream more vigorously.
	Insufficient beating-in of egg (this means mixture will curdle).	Beat for a longer time.
Whisked mixtures		
Close heavy texture.	Insufficient whisking of eggs and sugar.	Whisk for a longer time.
	Careless folding-in of flour.	Use more care.
Fruit cakes		
Sunken fruit.	Mixture too soft.	Add less liquid.
	Too much raising agent.	Measure accurately.
	Moving cake while cooking.	
	Oven too hot.	Reduce oven temperature.
Burnt top.	Cooked too long.	Decrease cooking time.
	Cooked too near top of oven.	Cook on a lower shelf.
	Oven too hot.	Reduce oven temperature.

Index